HUMAN RIGHTS & LIBERTY

by

Charlie Ogden

Crabtree Publishing Company
www.crabtreebooks.com
1-800-387-7650

Published in Canada
Crabtree Publishing
616 Welland Avenue
St. Catharines, ON
L2M 5V6

Published in the United States
Crabtree Publishing
PMB 59051
350 Fifth Ave, 59th Floor
New York, NY 10118

Published by Crabtree Publishing Company in 2017

First Published by Book Life in 2016
Copyright © 2017 Book Life

Author
Charlie Ogden

Editors
Grace Jones
Janine Deschenes
Ellen Rodger

Design
Drue Rintoul

Proofreader
Crystal Sikkens

**Production coordinator and
prepress technician (interior)**
Margaret Amy Salter

Prepress technician (covers)
Ken Wright

Print coordinator
Katherine Berti

Printed in Hong Kong/012017/BK20161024

Photographs

Shutterstock: Nadezda Murmakova: cover (bottom);
  Lizette Potgieter: page 6; OlegD: page 7; LMspencer: page 11
  (bottom left); Vlad Karavaev page 11 (top right); TonyV3112:
  page 13; sunsinger: page 18 (top); Daniel J. Rao: page 18
  (bottom); Everett Historical: page 22; Noppasin: page 23;
  S.Borisov: page 24; Alessia Pierdomenico: page 25; Shahid
  Khan: page 28 (inset); Sean Pavone: page 29 (top); Nadezda
  Murmakova: page 29 (bottom);

Wikimedia Commons: DeMarsico, Dick page 9

Cover Images
(Top) Statue of Liberty and the New York City Skyline
(Bottom) Aung San Suu Kyi is a human rights activist and
  Nobel Peace prize winner who, in 2015, became Burma's
  (Myanmar's) first openly elected leader in 25 years.

Library and Archives Canada Cataloguing in Publication

Ogden, Charlie, author
     Human rights and liberty / Charlie Ogden.

(Our values)
Issued in print and electronic formats.
ISBN 978-0-7787-3267-9 (hardback).--
ISBN 978-0-7787-3368-3 (paperback).--
ISBN 978-1-4271-1898-1 (html)

     1. Human rights--Juvenile literature. 2. Liberty--Juvenile
literature. I. Title.

JC571.O53 2016   j323   C2016-906668-1
                                      C2016-906669-X

Library of Congress Cataloging-in-Publication Data

CIP available at Library of Congress

CONTENTS

Words in **bold** can be found in the glossary on page 31.

WHAT ARE HUMAN RIGHTS?

There are certain things that people can do because the law allows them to, such as drive cars, watch television, and travel around the world. However, many people argue that there are certain things that people should always be allowed to do simply because they are human. These things are known as human rights. Human rights help people to live with freedom, equality, justice, and peace.

Not everyone agrees on what is and what isn't a human right. However, there are a few rights that most people agree everyone has simply because they are human. They are:

- The right to liberty
- The right to life
- The right to equality
- The right to a fair trial
- The right to freedom of speech
- The right to freedom of religion

Don't worry if you don't understand what these rights mean at the moment. We will talk about all of them later on!

SOME PEOPLE ARGUE THAT THERE ARE OVER 30 BASIC HUMAN RIGHTS.

Here are three Buddhists practicing their right to freedom of religion.

WHAT IS A RIGHT?

A right is something that someone has the authority, or permission, to have or do. A person might have permission to do something because the law says they can. This is called a legal right. For example, most adults have the legal right to vote. To vote is to have a say in who is part of your country's **government**. A person might also have permission to do something because it is the fair or right thing to do. This is called a moral right. For example, you have the moral right to tell a teacher about a bully.

Even though you may not know all of your human rights yet, they are still there. Even babies have human rights!

In many cases, a legal right is based on a moral right. One example of this is that it is illegal to steal. Many people believe that no one ever has the moral right to steal, so laws have been made that say no one ever has the legal right to steal either.

THERE ARE A LOT OF PEOPLE AROUND THE WORLD WHO ARE TRYING TO MAKE HAVING ACCESS TO THE INTERNET A HUMAN RIGHT.

THE RIGHT TO EQUALITY

Every person has the right to live in a society that promotes the equality of all people. Such a society views everyone as equally important, gives everyone the same rights, and allows everyone the same opportunities. The right to equality is very important because it states that all of the other human rights must be equally applied to everyone.

IN AFGHANISTAN, WOMEN ARE OFTEN NOT GVEN THE SAME OPPORTUNITIES AS MEN. FOR EXAMPLE, ONLY 17 PERCENT OF AFGHAN WOMEN ARE LITERATE, OR ARE ABLE TO READ AND WRITE, WHILE 51 PERCENT OF MEN ARE LITERATE.

Afghanistan

The right to equality has been one of the most difficult rights to protect because some cultures around the world do not consider everyone to be equal. Often women are not treated as equal to men, and are not allowed in some places to get an education or have a job. People who do not have their right to equality protected by their government can be made to feel rejected and powerless.

THE RIGHT TO FREEDOM OF RELIGION

The right to freedom of religion means that people can be free to practice their beliefs. In many places, people from different religions and faiths often live together very happily. In communities such as these, people **respect** a person's right to practice whatever religion they like. However, there are places in the world where the right to religious freedom isn't always respected, and people are forced to stop practicing their faith.

A person's right to freedom of religion is a very important right to respect. One of the reasons for this is because a person's **identity** can be very closely linked to their religion. People often make their faith a significant part of their lives. In these circumstances, if a person's right to freedom of religion isn't respected, it can threaten their sense of identity. A person should have the right to express their identity and beliefs.

THE MOST RELIGIOUSLY DIVERSE COUNTRY IN THE WORLD IS SINGAPORE, WHICH HAS LARGE POPULATIONS OF BUDDHISTS, CHRISTIANS, MUSLIMS, TAOISTS, AND HINDUS.

Singapore

These men are Hindus, which means they practice Hindu Dharma, or the duties of their faith.

THE RIGHT TO A FAIR TRIAL

The right to a fair trial is an important right for governments to respect because it protects people from being unfairly punished. When someone is accused of committing a crime in a country that respects the right to a fair trial, they will get the opportunity to defend themselves.

They can put forward evidence in court to prove that they didn't commit the crime. Court is a group of people brought together to decide on a crime. A judge and a **jury** will look at evidence and might agree that the person did not commit the crime, meaning that they won't be unfairly punished.

Respecting the right to a fair trial means that people have the right to be represented by a lawyer in court. A lawyer is a person who studies law and argues for a person in court.

In places where the right to a fair trial isn't respected, people are often punished as soon as they are accused of a crime. They aren't given a chance to defend themselves. This can lead to a lot of people being punished for crimes they haven't actually committed.

THE RIGHT TO FREEDOM OF SPEECH

The right to freedom of speech means that everyone should be able to voice their opinions in public. This is not limited to just speaking in public, but also includes writing your opinions in a book or even on the Internet. Freedom of speech protects a person's right to discuss their own opinions without being punished or **censored**. Freedom of speech is important because it allows people to point out inequities, or unfairness, in society and government. In this way, free speech is a peaceful weapon against **oppression** and **tyranny**. But free speech must not cross the line into **libel**, **slander**, or **hate speech** against a person or group. These things are against the law in many countries.

Martin Luther King Jr. made his famous "I Have a Dream" speech in 1963 and changed the way that people thought about equality in America. He could not have done this without his right to the freedom of speech.

THERE ARE MANY COUNTRIES IN THE WORLD WHERE PEOPLE DON'T HAVE THE RIGHT TO FREEDOM OF SPEECH, SUCH AS NORTH KOREA AND BURMA (ALSO KNOWN AS MYANMAR).

North Korea

Burma/ Myanmar

WHY ARE HUMAN RIGHTS IMPORTANT?

Human rights are important because they protect everyone. No matter who you are or where in the world you live, you are protected by human rights. Human rights protect people because they are universal and internationally guaranteed, which means that every government has to provide its citizens with human rights. Every human should have the same rights. But in some countries, governments and individuals violate human rights.

If something is universal it means that it applies to every person no matter where they live. Human rights are universal because they should apply to all people on Earth.

INTERNATIONAL GUARANTEE

Human rights are considered natural rights. These are rights that are unalienable, or cannot be taken away by governments. In 1948, the United Nations, or UN, was formed. It is an international organization that aims to protect human rights and foster international cooperation. The same year it was formed, the UN adopted the Universal Declaration of Human Rights (UDHR). The UDHR is the first global document to outline the natural rights of all citizens of the planet. It has 32 articles, including article 1 that says all humans are born free and equal in dignity and rights. Many countries signed the UDHR, but not all have respected human rights in practice.

South Sudan

MANY COUNTRIES IN AFRICA HAVE GOVERNMENTS THAT MAKE IT DIFFICULT FOR ORGANIZATIONS TO PROTECT THE HUMAN RIGHTS OF THEIR CITIZENS. EXAMPLES INCLUDE SOUTH SUDAN AND THE DEMOCRATIC REPUBLIC OF THE CONGO.

DR Congo

South Sudan

DR Congo

INFLUENCE ON GOVERNMENTS

Governments often create laws and policies based on human rights. The human right to life means that everyone has a right to food, water, and shelter since these are the basic things that people need in order to live. Many people are able to provide these things for themselves. However, in cases where people aren't able to provide these things for themselves, their government has a duty to provide these things for them. Governments are influenced by human rights because they have a responsibility to make sure that the fundamental rights of all of the people in their country are being respected and protected.

IN MANY WEALTHIER COUNTRIES, THE RIGHT TO A BASIC INCOME IS CONSIDERED A HUMAN RIGHT. SOME COUNTRIES PROVIDE THIS THROUGH SOCIAL WELFARE OR SOCIAL SECURITY PROGRAMS. THESE PROGRAMS ARE MEANT TO ENSURE PEOPLE, INCLUDING CHILDREN AND RETIRED SENIORS, HAVE THEIR BASIC NEEDS MET.

Human rights also prevent governments from having too much power over the public. They prevent governments from stopping people from having children, not giving people a fair trial in court, and using people as slaves, among other things. Since human rights are universal, these things shouldn't ever happen to anyone. However, not every government respects universal human rights.

Today, human rights are widely accepted and protected. There are many international human rights treaties and laws that support human rights throughout the world. Treaties are agreements made between governments. These treaties are sometimes used to threaten a government that is violating human rights. For example, if a government was found to be using the people in its country as slaves, other governments and organizations would use these treaties to try to stop that practice.

WHAT IS LIBERTY?

One of the most important human rights is the right to liberty because it gives people freedom. This right states that all people can choose how they live their lives. It means that people have the freedom to choose what they wear, what they eat, where they live, and where they work. Unfortunately, governments do not always respect every person's right to liberty. Some governments **detain** and imprison people without a legal reason. Some do not allow people to move freely within the country.

Part of the right to liberty is being able to choose where you live.

14

During the first few years of every person's life, they do not have the right to liberty, even though they have many other rights. Children do not usually have the right to choose where they live or what they eat. A child's parents or guardians decide this. In most countries, people don't have the right to liberty until they reach a specific age.

TODAY, OVER 10 MILLION PEOPLE AROUND THE WORLD ARE IN PRISON. OVER 2 MILLION OF THESE PRISONERS ARE IN THE UNITED STATES, MAKING IT THE COUNTRY WITH THE HIGHEST NUMBER OF PRISONERS IN THE WORLD.

Another example of people who don't have the right to liberty are prisoners. Convicted prisoners lose their right to liberty when they are sentenced to prison for a crime. Although they do not have the right to choose where they live, prisoners still have other human rights. Most are not taken away just because they are imprisoned.

WHY IS LIBERTY IMPORTANT?

Liberty is one of our most basic needs as human beings. The right to liberty is sometimes considered a natural desire by humans. The earliest humans had complete freedom over their lives before governments and **empires** that ruled over other people were established. When a person does not have liberty, they can feel powerless. Liberty gives a person freedom, but not at the expense of the rights of others. It's important to remember that although everyone should have the right to liberty, it does not mean complete freedom that would interfere with other people's human rights.

THE STATUE OF LIBERTY, WHICH STANDS IN NEW YORK HARBOR, IS A SYMBOL OF THE LIBERTY OF THE AMERICAN PEOPLE.

LIFE, LIBERTY, AND HAPPINESS

The idea of liberty is often linked to happiness. In fact, the two words make up part of the best-known phrase from the United States Declaration of Independence: "Life, Liberty, and the pursuit of Happiness." These three things are considered unalienable rights, or natural rights that everyone should have. Liberty means unbounded or unrestricted. Freedom means the power to act, think, or speak freely, or without restraint. Many countries have constitutions and human rights charters, which are documents that outline rights. Many contain the words life and liberty.

THE WORLD HAPPINESS REPORT HAS SHOWN THAT THE HAPPIEST COUNTRIES IN THE WORLD, WHICH ARE DENMARK, SWITZERLAND, AND ICELAND, ARE ALSO THE COUNTRIES WHERE CITIZENS HAVE THE GREATEST AMOUNT OF LIBERTY.

This is Copenhagen, the capital city of Denmark.

IMPROVING SOCIETY

Many people argue that the importance of liberty is mostly related to the positive effect it has on people and the communities they live in. When everyone is free to pursue their goals and interests, a community becomes a happier, more vibrant place.

People who have the liberty to start businesses, create art, and try new things bring life and color to their communities. In a community where liberty is respected, people can learn from each other and follow their individual goals and dreams.

These women in India have formed a collective to farm and sell rice in their communities. A collective is a cooperative business or organization. The women have the liberty to pursue their skills and interests.

It's important to remember that liberty is slightly different than total freedom. A community can only be made better by liberty if individual liberties do not hurt the rights of other people. Liberty means that people have freedoms, such as the freedom of religion or the freedom of speech, but the rights of other people limit these freedoms. In many countries, people have the right to not be discriminated against based on their **race**, **gender**, age, physical ability, and more. They are protected against these kinds of discrimination under the laws in their countries. This means that if a person wants to practice their liberty, they cannot do so in a way that discriminates against other people. A person can't use their freedom of speech to say hateful things against someone's race, or treat someone unfairly at work based on their religion. Doing so may be considered hate speech, which in some countries is against the law.

HUMAN RIGHTS AND LIBERTY
IN HISTORY

ATHENS

Liberty has been seen as a human right since the time of the ancient Greeks. One city in particular, Athens, is noted for giving its citizens more liberty than any other country did for hundreds of years after. Although Athens is now the capital city of Greece, 2,500 years ago it was an **independent** city that acted much like a country does today.

ATHENS WAS NAMED AFTER ATHENA, THE GREEK GODDESS OF WISDOM AND JUSTICE.

This is the Parthenon, an ancient temple in Athens dedicated to Athena.

Athens was certainly ahead of its time, but it was not perfect. While rich men had liberty, not everyone else in the city was as lucky. Women had very little freedom and were dependent on the goodwill of their male family members. Many wealthy people in Athens had slaves to do their work. These slaves had no liberty and were forced to follow the will of their owners.

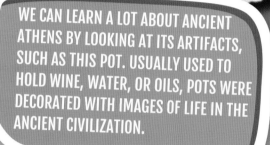

Athens, the capital city of Greece

WE CAN LEARN A LOT ABOUT ANCIENT ATHENS BY LOOKING AT ITS ARTIFACTS, SUCH AS THIS POT. USUALLY USED TO HOLD WINE, WATER, OR OILS, POTS WERE DECORATED WITH IMAGES OF LIFE IN THE ANCIENT CIVILIZATION.

Democracy is an ancient Greek word that translates roughly as "people power." Ancient Greece is known as the birthplace of democracy, a system of government where leaders are elected by citizens. Voting is one expression of liberty because it allows free choice in government representation. Although ancient Greece had democracy, only adult male citizens who owned land could vote.

LIBERTY IN THE UNITED STATES

The Charters of Freedom are three of the most important documents establishing personal freedom and government responsibility in the United States. They include the Declaration of Independence, written in 1776, the Constitution, enacted in 1789, and the Bill of Rights—amendments to the Constitution that were added over time, beginning in 1789. The Charters of Freedom are documents that embrace the ideas of liberty and equality. They were written during the Age of Enlightenment, a time when these ideas were new. At the time, people began to reject absolute monarchy in favor of freedom of speech, religion, the press, and civil rights. They began to see individuals, and not just kings and nobles, as having natural rights to liberty.

"We hold these truths to be self-evident, that all men are created equal, that they are endowed by their Creator with certain unalienable rights, that among these are life, liberty, and the pursuit of happiness."

The Declaration of Independence was written to give America, which at the time had only thirteen states, independence from Great Britain.

WORLD WAR II

Human rights did not fully grow into the idea that we know today until after World War II. This war lasted from 1939 to 1945 and involved many of the most powerful countries in the world at the time. It was a brutal war with so many atrocities. It made people begin to think that establishing basic human rights might protect people from atrocities in the future. The biggest atrocity during World War II, called the Holocaust, made many people support the idea of universal human rights. The Holocaust is the name given to the genocide of six million European Jews at the hands of the Nazi regime and its collaborators. Genocide is the deliberate killing of a large group of people of a specific group with the intent to end the existence of the group. Until 1944, there was no word to describe this type of mass murder. Giving it a name helped give the human rights movement a common purpose: to prevent future genocides.

DURING THE HOLOCAUST, MILLIONS OF JEWS, AS WELL AS ROMA, GAY PEOPLE, COMMUNISTS, AND OTHERS WERE TARGETED BECAUSE OF THEIR RACE, ETHNICITY, RELIGION, AND PERSONAL BELIEFS.

The Holocaust memorial in Berlin, Germany, commemorates all of the lives lost during the Holocaust and serves as a reminder of the importance of universal human rights.

UNITED NATIONS

An organization made up of governments from all around the world was established immediately after World War II. It was established to promote cooperation between countries and to prevent a war like World War II from ever happening again. The organization is known as the United Nations, often just called the UN for short, and it is still very important today. The UN composed the Universal Declaration of Human Rights in 1948. This declaration was signed by 48 different countries and includes all the rights talked about at the beginning of this book, as well as many others. Many consider this declaration to be part of international law, meaning that all of the countries who signed it have an obligation to respect and protect the human rights of everyone on the planet.

THE UNITED NATIONS WAS ESTABLISHED TO REPLACE A PREVIOUS ORGANIZATION CALLED THE LEAGUE OF NATIONS.

The United Nations created the Universal Declaration of Human Rights in Paris, France on December 10, 1948.

After the Universal Declaration of Human Rights was signed, many countries improved their position on human rights.

However, it took some countries a lot longer than others.

NELSON MANDELA WAS THE FIRST BLACK PRESIDENT OF SOUTH AFRICA. HE SPENT 27 YEARS IN PRISON FOR TRYING TO PROMOTE EQUALITY IN HIS COUNTRY.

This is the flag of South Africa.

One country that took many years to begin respecting human rights was South Africa. South Africa did not sign the Universal Declaration of Human Rights in 1948 because its system, called apartheid, did not respect human rights. Apartheid was a complex system of **racial segregation** and **economic oppression** that classified people according to race.

It forced black, mixed race, and people of East Indian descent to live in designated areas apart from white people. Clearly, the South African government at the time did not respect its citizens' right to liberty. Apartheid began to be dismantled in 1990. In 1994, a new government, led by Nelson Mandela, was elected and more freedoms were enacted.

HUMAN RIGHTS AND LIBERTY TODAY

Today, many countries have laws that protect the human rights of the people who live there. In the United States, human rights are protected under the United States Constitution. Among other things, the Constitution protects the right to freedom of religion, freedom of speech, and the right to petition, which means to formally complain against something. It also gives people the right to a fair trial and the right to vote. In Canada, the Canadian Human Rights Commission is an organization that works to make sure every person's human rights are protected. The Human Rights Act in Canada means that the government is obligated to protect the rights of all citizens. The Act makes it illegal to discriminate against people based on such things as race, gender, age, and ability.

> CANADA AND SAN MARINO ARE CONSIDERED BY MANY PEOPLE TO HAVE SOME OF THE BEST HUMAN RIGHTS LAWS IN THE WORLD.

San Marino

Canada

San Marino

While the state of human rights in the world is much better today than it has ever been in history, there is still a long way to go. This becomes very clear when we think about modern slavery. While no one is certain about the exact number, most people agree that there are more than 25 million slaves in the world today. Many of these people were promised paid work in foreign countries, but when they arrived in these countries they were forced to work for nothing. Slaves today often have to work far away from their homes and families, and they have little hope of escaping the slavery that they have been forced into.

THERE ARE ROUGHLY 14 MILLION PEOPLE TRAPPED IN SLAVERY IN INDIA TODAY, WHICH IS MORE THAN ANY OTHER COUNTRY IN THE WORLD.

India

MUNSHIGHAT मुंशी घाट

Varanasi, India, is one of the oldest cities in the world.

27

HUMAN RIGHTS
CASE STUDIES

MALALA YOUSAFZAI

Today, in Pakistan, the human right to equality is not respected, and many women do not have the same right to education as men. In 2009, Malala Yousafzai began speaking out against the lack of education for girls in her country and the need for her right to go to school to be protected. Malala's activism made her a target of the Taliban, an extremist Muslim religious group that is opposed to education for girls and women. In 2012, Malala was shot on her way home from school by a Taliban gunman. The group wanted to silence the 15-year-old girl.

IN 2014, MALALA YOUSAFZAI WAS AWARDED THE NOBEL PEACE PRIZE, MAKING HER THE YOUNGEST PERSON TO EVER RECEIVE THE AWARD.

Luckily, Malala survived the attack and has since moved to the United Kingdom, where she has continued her education. Malala is seen by many as a symbol of equality and human rights.

Malala Yousafzai.

This is the Swat Valley in Pakistan, where Malala lived before moving to the United Kingdom. It is too dangerous for she and her family to return.

AUNG SAN SUU KYI

Aung San Suu Kyi is a human rights activist and Nobel Peace prize winner who, in 2015, became Burma's (Myanmar's) first openly elected leader in 25 years. Aung had been arrested in 1989 for organizing peaceful protests and criticizing the government for not respecting the human rights of its citizens, among other things. Aung was put under house arrest, meaning that she wasn't allowed to leave her house, for nearly 15 years. Throughout her arrest, she persisted in pushing for human rights and democracy in her country.

Shwedagon Pagoda in Yangon, Myanmar

AFTER HER RELEASE FROM HOUSE ARREST IN 2010, AUNG CONTINUED TO PRESS FOR DEMOCRACY. SHE WAS ELECTED TO THE BURMA (MYANMAR PARLIAMENT IN 2012 AND WAS ELECTED LEADER IN 2015.

Burma (Myanmar) has been led by a brutal government for so long, many people do not understand what human rights for all means. Aung San Suu Kyi's government must now try to make people in her country reject conflict and violence.

Aung San Suu Kyi

THINK ABOUT IT!

1 Think about the human rights you have learned about in this book. What do you think is the most important human right? Why do you think so?

Right to Life

2 Think about the human rights that you are entitled to, such as your liberty or your freedom of speech and religion. How do you express them?

Right to Liberty

3 Many countries still do not respect the human rights of its citizens, and many people live without the right to liberty. Why do you think it is important for all people to have the right to liberty?

Right to a Fair Trial

Right to Freedom of Speech

Right to Equality

Right to Freedom of Religion

GLOSSARY

absolute monarchy A form of government in which a monarch (usually a king or queen) has complete power

atrocities Extremely cruel acts

censored To have an opinion suppressed or hidden by an authority

collaborators A person or group who cooperate or work together with an enemy

communists A person who believes in communism, a theory that supports the idea that people should all have equal power and property in a society

constitution A collection of rules that state how a government should work or run

democracy A type of government in which power is given to the people

detain To keep someone in custody of a government

economic oppression The unfair treatment of someone through slavery, low wages, denial of job opportunity, and other forms of discrimination based on economics

empire The land or people under control of another country

gay people People who are homosexual, or attracted to others of the same sex

gender How a person feels about their identity and expresses themselves. There are many genders, not limited to male and female.

government The group of people with the authority to run a country

hate speech Speech that discriminates against or encourages violence against a person or group. It is illegal in varying degrees in many countries.

identity A person's view of who they are

independent Not ruled by another country

Jews People who follow the religion of Judaism

jury A group of people who decide whether someone has committed a crime

libel The crime of writing a false statement that damages another's reputation

Nazi regime The government controlled by Adolf Hitler and the Nazi Party, who had absolute control over Germany and facilitated the Holocaust

obligation Something that a person is morally or legally required to do

oppression Cruel or unjust treatment of a person or group for a long period of time

race Usually defined as the division of people based on similar physical characteristics, coming from common ancestry

racial segregation Separated or divided based on race

respect To think about others' feelings and give something the attention it deserves

Roma One of several names used to describe the ethnic group known as the Romanies or "Gypsies," which is considered derogatory

slander The crime of making a false statement that damages another's reputation

tyranny Oppressive government or use of power

INDEX